You're On
A Mission
A 31-Day Devotional
Journey Around the World

Published by

NEW DIRECTIONS
INTERNATIONAL

PO Box 2347
Burlington, NC 27216-2347
www.newdirections.org

ISBN: 978-159858-417-2
Library of Congress Control Number is applied for.

Ministry contact: ndi@newdirections.org

Printed in the United States of America.

Cover design and layout by Vincent Graves

New Directions International is an evangelical missions organization that connects
followers of Christ with strategic leaders overseas to help fulfill the Great Commission.

This book is in honor of
the faithful friends and partners
who have made NDI an effective ministry
for God's glory since 1968.

Contents

Foreword

The biggest difference between Christianity and all other world religions is the incarnation - God taking bodily form. Or as the Apostle John explained this miracle: "The Word became flesh and made His dwelling among us" (John 1:14). No other religion reveals a god who came to earth and took upon Himself our nature so that we in turn could take His nature upon ourselves.

This is at the heart of Christianity, why the Gospel is constantly referred to in the Bible as "good news." It's the revelation of the invisible God making Himself visible, available, knowable, and loveable. That's why John could say the unthinkable about God in Christ: "we have heard...we have seen with our eyes...we have looked at and our hands have touched...the Word of life" (I John 1:1).

This 31 day devotional book is a continuation of that incarnation through the lives of God's people in many countries of the world. These are not just stories we have heard from others. They are not second-hand accounts or hearsay. I personally know most of the people whom you will meet in this book. They are dear friends and partners of us here at New Directions International. In their own way, each is an incarnation of the love, mercy, and grace of the Lord Jesus. I can't wait for you to meet them in the following pages.

Your next month with these people can change your life forever! Their stories will personalize missions for you in a way that you perhaps have never experienced before. So begin reading now and meet some very special people whose commitment to Christ has deeply impacted my life and the ministry of NDI!

Dr. J.L. Williams
Founder and Chief Ministry Officer
New Directions International

Introduction

There is a stigma around the word "mission" or "missions." In the minds of Westerners it conjures up images of selling everything you own, moving to some distant continent, and living among half-naked cannibals who've never seen an outsider. I think you would agree that there are very few people who would get excited about this kind of journey into the unknown and untamed wild.

Perhaps for this or some other reason you are just not interested in missions. You might think that God hasn't called you to help spread the Gospel, whether it's going on a short-term trip overseas or giving money for someone you know to go. You believe it's someone else's job to reach the unsaved in other countries. We have enough lost people to deal with here in our own country, right?

No matter what your opinion of missions is, let me encourage you to dwell on Jesus' words in Acts 1:8: "You will be my witnesses in Jerusalem, and in all Judea and Samaria, and to the ends of the earth." In other words, you need to be a witness for Him in your hometown *and* around the world.

Jesus put it in even simpler words in Matthew 28:19: "Go and make disciples of all nations." He didn't add a disclaimer to this sentence like "go unless you can convince someone else to" or "make disciples only if you want to." As the pioneer missionary Hudson Taylor once said, "The Great Commission is not an option to be considered; it is a command to be obeyed."

The thought of reaching lost people for Jesus should be an exciting thought for every follower of Christ. Can you imagine the angelic celebration in heaven every time someone accepts Jesus Christ as their Lord and Savior?! You will find great joy being a part of this eternal process.

As you read this devotional over the next month, you are going to read some amazing stories. I hope that you will be encouraged and motivated – encouraged by what you'll read each day, and motivated to apply the practical and spiritual lessons to your life.

Christ's Great Commission directs you to share His love with those around you. It all starts right there in your home, on your street, in your neighborhood, in your city. But it doesn't have to stop there. You can pray for the lost, give for missions work through your church or an organization like NDI, share with others about the needs, or go yourself. Then you will live a life of growing eternal significance.

You're On A Mission.

In God's Time

Day 1

Bhaktapur, Nepal

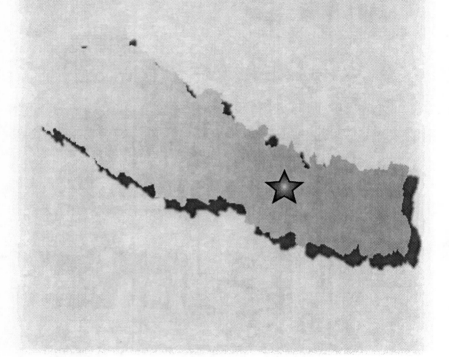

Photo Description

Pastor Tir Dewan suffered with the lasting effects of the physical persecution - specifically head trauma - that he endured before Nepal became a democracy.

In God's Time

As the heavens are higher than the earth, so are My ways higher than your ways and My thoughts than your thoughts.

Isaiah 55:9

In our land of fast food, fast cars, and fast living, it is hard to be patient. We want our meals now, to get where we're going now, and our needs met NOW. This impatience can spill over into our prayer life. We might pray once for something, but quickly give up if the Lord doesn't answer us according to our timetable.

Can you imagine praying diligently for 40 years before the Lord answered your prayer? Pastor Tir Dewan's desire was to have a permanent church building in which to worship. For years his congregation moved from one rented room to another in Nepal. In addition, he was beaten and imprisoned many times for his faith. Yet he never gave up and never stopped praying.

The Lord answered Pastor Dewan's prayer when he was 86 years old! A family here in America came alongside this pastor and church, and provided the necessary funds for this congregation to have their own permanent building in which to worship. God honored Pastor Dewan's prayers and answered in His time before this dear old pastor's time on earth was through.

We may never understand the delays that God seems to take in answering our prayers. This verse in Isaiah, however, reminds us that we probably won't understand because His ways are higher than ours. Our finite minds cannot grasp the ways of the infinite God. So believe by faith that God hears your prayers, and He will answer them in His time according to His will.

Prayer

Father, help me to be diligent in my prayers, especially for the salvation of family and friends. Remind me that my perseverance in prayer can make a difference in where they spend eternity! Please call them to Yourself in Your time.

A Large Need

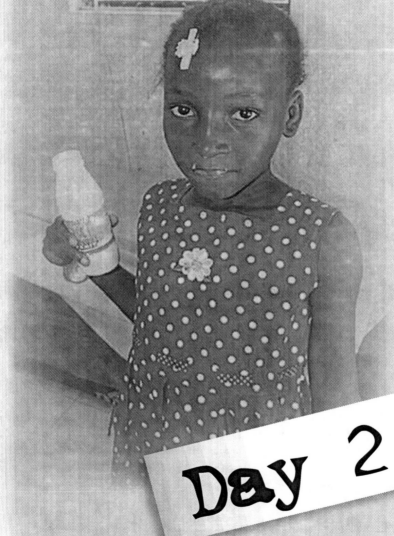

Day 2

Croix des Bouquets, Haiti

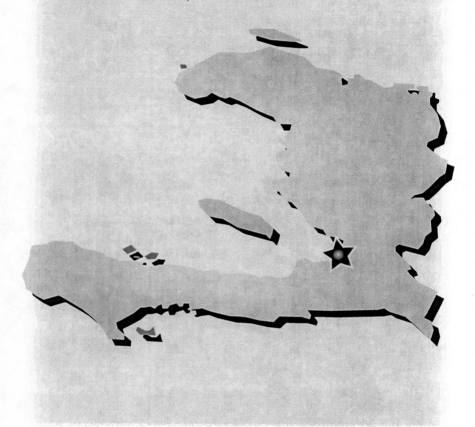

Photo Description
A girl in a Haitian children's home gets an unexpected gift of milk. She is standing in front of one of the "beds" – porous air mattresses placed on benches.

A Large Need

Do not take advantage of a widow or an orphan.
If you do and they cry out to me, I will certainly hear their cry.

Exodus 22:22-23

Fifty-six orphans shared one simple house in Haiti. There was clean water from a well, which was wonderful, but only one bag of rice to be found in the house and not much else. There were no chairs, no tables, and no beds. Those who didn't sleep on the floor pushed four or five benches together and covered them with a flat air mattress. The mattresses had several holes, so it wouldn't hold air.

Two girls in particular stood out to the visiting mission team. They were nine and ten years old, but actually looked like they were half that age. Both would have found some milk to be a treasure, but even more so, they just desired attention. The team took great joy in bringing a smile to the children that day, and left praying about how to help this orphans' home.

Anyone who has traveled overseas to do mission work can find similar scenarios like this all around the world. Orphans (and widows) are the most discarded and least cared for people on earth. There are well over 100 million orphans worldwide, including an estimated 15 million AIDS orphans.

How can you help a need that is so large? The above verse gives us hope that the Lord has not forgotten these precious little souls. Through feeding and literacy programs as well as orphan homes, everyone should be doing something to help them. Pray that the Lord would rescue them, and that followers of Christ would find ways to get involved in meeting the needs of orphans through worthy missions organizations and charities.

Prayer

God, please help me hear the cry of needy orphans around the world who are hungry and suffering. Provide for them through Your people and save them from a hopeless eternity.

Where Is Your Treasure?

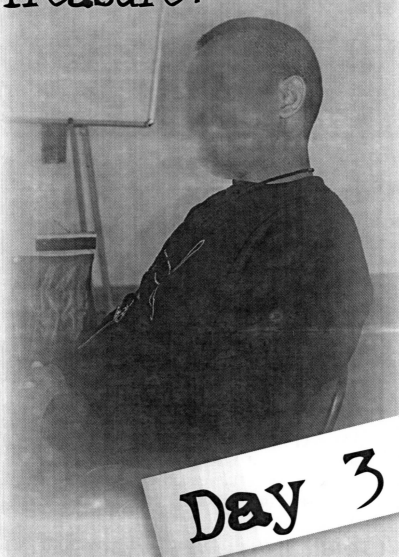

Day 3

Bhutan-India Border

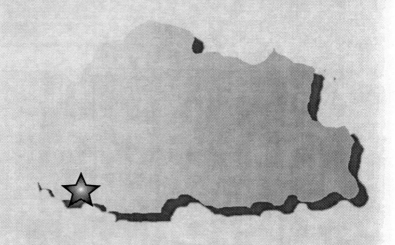

Photo Description

Since Bhutan is a closed country to the Gospel, many
ministries like "Daniel's" (*identity protected*) are located
along the Bhutan-India border.

Where Is Your Treasure?

Do not store up for yourselves treasures on earth, where moth and rust destroy, and where thieves break in and steal. But store up for yourselves treasures in heaven, where moth and rust do not destroy, and where thieves do not break in and steal.

Matthew 6:19-20

D epending on where you go in the world, the names and forms that money take may change, but its gripping effect on mankind always remains the same. "Daniel" was raised in Bhutan as a Buddhist. He decided as a young man to start his own business in order to accumulate wealth.

It was during this time that Daniel came into contact with a group of men involved in illegal business activities. Seeing this as an opportunity to increase his wealth, he decided to join this group of men. Daniel was on the track toward amassing a great fortune – so he thought.

In a matter of months, he was completely bankrupt and dependent on his family to cover his debts and provide for his needs. A burden to his family, Daniel was sent into the military where the seeds of Christ were first planted in him. Today, Daniel has traded in a life bent on storing up treasures on earth for a life spent on storing up treasures in heaven. He ministers inside the borders of Bhutan to expand God's Kingdom.

The Scriptures are consistent in communicating that it is futile to be lovers of money. No matter how much wealth one amasses, money is temporal. Eventually, the fortune will be spent or we will pass away and not be able to spend it. Investing in the things of the Lord is an eternal investment, which affords benefits in heaven. Be

21

ızes that money can secure for you do not distract
prize, Christ Jesus.

Prayer

*Father, forgive me when I have made the pursuit of money and
material possessions more important than my relationship with
You. Help me to keep my focus on activities and actions
that have eternal value.*

The Importance of Perseverance

Day 4

Kathmandu, Nepal

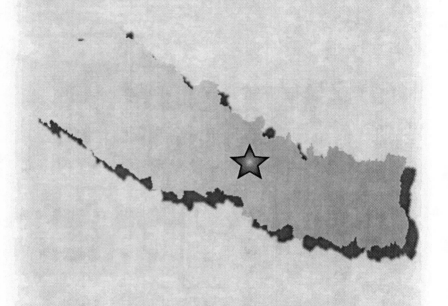

Photo Description

Ratna Rai has defied the odds as a paraplegic – but only because the Body of Christ came alongside his family. This is what Christian love is all about.

The Importance of Perseverance

We know that suffering produces perseverance; perseverance, character, and character, hope.

Romans 5:3-4

Ratna Rai had long lived among the ranks of the unemployed. Being a paraplegic, he had little or no way to provide for his wife and three children - one of which is a deaf-mute. As a result, he had to endure a hard life of living in a wheelchair and fighting against poverty.

Ratna managed to get by with the help of family and through the outreach, provision, and love of a church in Kathmandu, Nepal. He was discipled through the church and grew strong in his witness for Christ. Through the church's pastor, Ratna and his family's plight were brought to the attention of NDI.

As a result, the family moved into a modest home built for them. Ratna and his family were set up with a small candle-making business that has not only helped to make him become self-sufficient, but helped to pay for the home's construction as well. His children were also helped with their everyday and educational needs. Perseverance has produced the fruit of strong character and hope in Christ for Ratna and his entire family!

You may feel like "fate" has dealt you a tough hand. You might be facing a long-term or permanent health problem, job insecurity, or strained family relations. As the verse in Romans shows us, what starts in suffering can end in hope *if* you keep your eyes on the

Savior who loves you. If you do this, you will also develop the perseverance necessary to not only survive, but also thrive.

Prayer

Gracious heavenly Father, grant me the perseverance through the trials and tribulations that You allow in my life. I want to reap the fruit of a strong character, as well as enduring hope in Christ my Savior!

To the End

Day 5

Your Town, USA

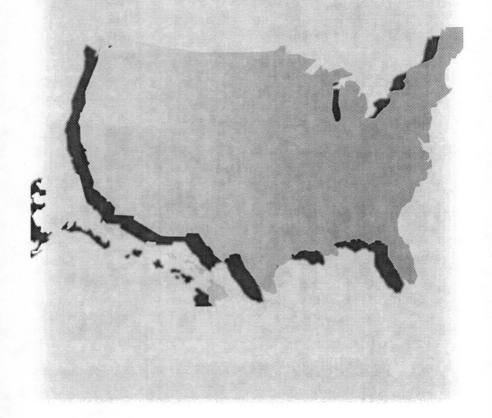

Photo Description
In addition to being NDI's Board Chairman, Wes Morgan was NDI's Volunteer Coordinator for Haiti, visiting and leading mission teams into the country dozens of times.

To the End

Make the most of every opportunity.

Colossians 4:5

It is a common misconception that evangelism and the mission field are overseas in some foreign country. It's also right here at home. NDI's former Board Chairman, Wes Morgan, had a difficult struggle with cancer for two and a half years until the Lord took him home. He once wrote to me, "I would go through all of this if it resulted in one person being saved for eternity." Well, I know at least one person who was.

Our son, Nathan, had been praying for Wes from time to time. As my wife, Susannah, and I were talking with Nathan in his bed just before prayer time, I told him that Wes wasn't doing well. He was concerned that Wes was going to die, and he began to cry. This turned into further discussion between Nathan and Susannah about our mortality, and how death is not the end if we have Jesus in our heart.

Nathan first asked Jesus into his heart on June 29, 2005 when he was almost four years old. We reminded him of this, but he did not remember, now at five and a half years old. So we walked him through the plan of salvation again, and he repeated the prayer that I prayed, inviting Jesus into his heart a second time, hopefully at an age that he will remember.

We hoped that a day like this would come, as we knew he would need additional spiritual markers in his life since he was so young the first time he prayed. The Lord used Wes' pain and suffering for His glory by assuring my son's place in eternity.

Whether in sickness or health, in your town or around the world, the Lord wants us to be ready to witness to those around us. We need to be a faithful witness to the very end of our lives.

Prayer

God, may I be a witness for You to the end of my earthly life.
I submit my life to You again now.
Use me for Your glory, and use me to reach out to the lost.

Love Your Enemies

Day 6

South Horr, Kenya

Photo Description

Stakwell Yurenimo was recently married to Francesca, who is from the Rendille Tribe. In 2007 they had their first child, a daughter named Wendy.

Love Your Enemies

You have heard that it was said, "Love your neighbor and hate your enemy." But I tell you: Love your enemies and pray for those who persecute you.

Matthew 5:43-44

In Africa, the division among tribes is at least as hostile as the division among races has been in America. Stakwell Yurenimo is a former *moran* or warrior of the Samburu tribe in Northern Kenya. While enrolled in a high school program aimed at reconciling tribal relationships, Stakwell was forced to room with a member from his main rival tribe, the Turkana. It had been ingrained in him to hate the Turkana, so Stakwell made his roommate's life as miserable as possible by sabotaging or destroying his property.

One day during a soccer match, Stakwell knocked his roommate to the ground and kicked him in the face with the intention of breaking his neck. Instead, he knocked out all of the Turkana's front teeth. Stakwell faced certain suspension. However, the Turkana was a follower of Christ, and he went to the administration and asked them not to suspend Stakwell or make him pay for the dental work. He forgave Stakwell just as Christ had forgiven the Turkana!

Stakwell's heart was softened and he soon surrendered his life to Jesus Christ, which resulted in his family disowning him. Today, Stakwell has a sports ministry that reaches out to all of the tribes of Northern Kenya. Soccer teams from the various tribes are now playing each other with good sportsmanship, and are hearing the

Gospel as well!

It is part of our sinful nature that leads us to hate our neighbor based on social, racial, or religious factors. As new creations in Christ, however, we now have the capacity to sincerely love our neighbors even if they are our most bitter enemies.

Prayer

Lord, please give me a genuine love for people that I find difficult to love. Show me a way to practically demonstrate the love of Christ to those around me.

Watch Out!

Day 7

Victoria Falls, Zimbabwe

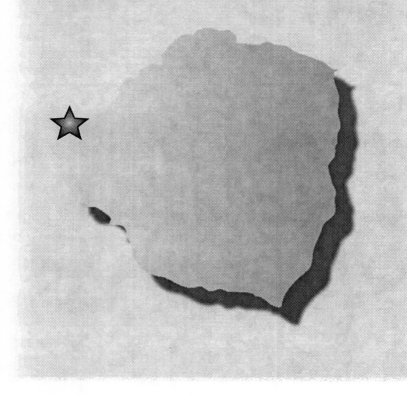

Photo Description
Wildlife often poses a danger to pastors and evangelists who are doing ministry in rural and unreached areas.

Watch Out!

The highway of the upright avoids evil; he who guards his way guards his life.

Proverbs 16:17

For the first five years I was on staff with NDI, my job was video production. I got a chance to travel frequently and see the world from the Taj Mahal in India to the bush of Kenya. On one particular mission trip to Zimbabwe, we were visiting one of our longtime partners to dedicate some churches near Victoria Falls, one of the seven natural wonders of the world.

Near one of the most beautiful spots on earth, in the midst of a break in the schedule, I was videotaping some elephants that were passing behind our hotel. As I was focusing on one particular elephant, I suddenly had the urge to stop what I was doing and turn around. There is no other way to describe it than that a sense of alarm came over me.

Hitting the pause button on the camcorder, I turned around and saw one of the adult elephants coming right at me – only 20 feet away and closing in steadily. He didn't look too happy! I proceeded to back pedal smoothly yet swiftly as I gave the great creature the space he was asking for. I often look back with regret that I didn't recognize the danger in the first place, but also with gratitude for the Lord warning me in my spirit of the peril I would have certainly faced.

Like this territorial elephant, sin can work in much the same way. If we are not aware of the threats and pitfalls around us, we may not recognize the danger in time. It is better that we be on our guard, and not put ourselves in compromising situations. The path God has laid out for us is narrow, but it can be found and navigated successfully if we focus on the Lord.

Prayer

Father, thank You for providing me with an escape from temptation and evil. Help me to be ever mindful of the danger of sin around me. Rescue me when I'm in the tough and compromising situations of life.

Thirst for the Word

Day 8

Sudan

Photo Description
While NDI and other organizations continue with spiritual, humanitarian, and development efforts, the persecution and genocide continues in Sudan.

Thirst for the Word

As the deer pants for streams of water, so my soul pants for You, O God.

Psalm 42:1

For many Christians around the world the Bible truly is their most treasured possession – if they even own one. We have heard stories of entire villages with only one copy, people making written copies, friends dividing the Bible up to read and then trade, and memorizing large portions of Scripture due to persecution and the unavailability of Bibles. The cost of getting one in a country hostile to the Gospel is not usually measured by monetary means, but personal safety. It is worth the risk to these Christians because it is the ultimate spiritual weapon.

NDI had the opportunity to airlift some Bibles into an unstable area of war-torn Sudan. Upon arrival on the ground, people appeared from all directions to see why the plane had come. When the Bible distribution began, there were hands everywhere, reaching for this precious gift written in the Nuer language. In particular, one middle-aged man wearing tattered clothing was most thankful. He told the mission team that this was the first whole Bible he had ever seen!

Is your Bible your most treasured possession? What a gift the Lord has given to each of us since it was completed almost 2,000 years ago! His word gives continual inspiration, as the Holy Spirit constantly guides and directs us.

Here in America, it is easy to take the availability of the Bible for granted. We have access to so many Bibles: paperback, hardback, Bibles with study guides, Bibles just for women or men, many different versions – all readily available. But if you don't read it, then it becomes just another book on the shelf. Make the message of Colossians 3:16 true for your life: "Let the words of Christ dwell in you richly."

Prayer

Thank you, Lord, for giving the gift of Your written word to me. Help me to develop the discipline of studying and meditating on it daily.

Where Are Your Feet Leading You?

Day 9

India

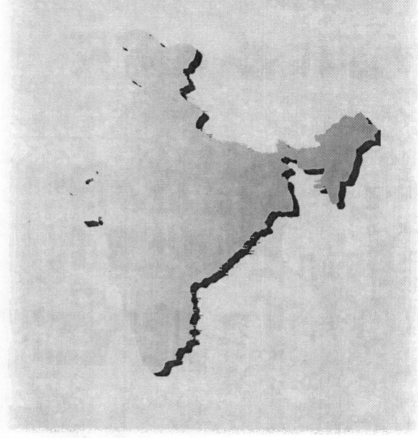

Photo Description
Sundar Singh's wholehearted devotion to the Lord has served as an example to many followers of Christ in India and around the world.

Where Are Your Feet Leading You?

*How beautiful on the mountains are the feet of those who bring
good news!*

Isaiah 52:7

Sundar Singh was born in Punjab, north India over a
century ago. His mother was a deeply religious woman
who nurtured Sundar in the noble traditions of the
Sikhs.

Miraculously converted to Christianity as a teenager,
then expelled from his family, Sundar took on the life of a sadhu
– someone who forsakes all worldly pleasure and devotes his life
to his religious beliefs. Sundar traveled all over India, Nepal, Tibet,
and other parts of the world. Armed with only his robe and New
Testament, he lived on the charity of others.

"I am not worthy to follow in the steps of my Lord," he said, "but,
like Him, I want no home, no possessions. Like Him I will belong to
the road, sharing the suffering of my people, eating with those who
will give me shelter, and telling all men of the love of God."

It wasn't long before Sundar developed a reputation as "the
apostle with the bleeding feet" because the soles of his feet were often
covered in bloody blisters. In 1929, he visited Tibet and was never
seen again. Yet his testimony lives on, showing that Christianity is
not an imported, foreign religion but is indigenous to Indian needs,
aspirations, and faith.

There are many followers of Christ around the world today that have lived the same simple life of sacrifice as Sundar did in order to share the love of Christ with others. People like Simon Mkolo who has planted hundreds of churches by walking from village to village in Zimbabwe, or Dinesh and Gyane Sunuwar who are trekking for days at a time to plant churches in the villages that lead up to Mt. Everest in Nepal.

How far are you willing to go to share the Gospel with those around you? God needs you to get on your feet and tell the story of His love for others. So let your feet do the walking and the Holy Spirit do the talking through you!

Prayer

Almighty Father, please use me today to share Your hope with those for whom You have burdened my heart, whether they are across the street or across the sea. I am available.

The Worldwide Body of Christ

Day 10

Kenya, Zimbabwe, and South Africa

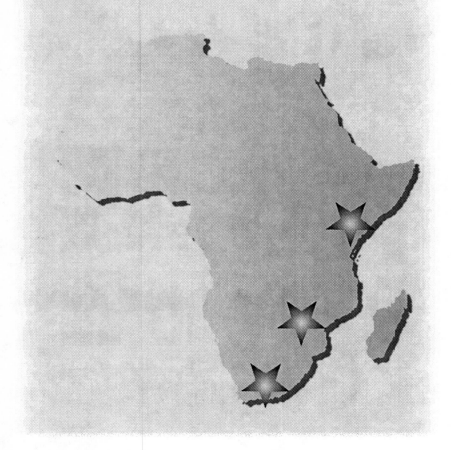

Photo Description
Four years after Scott Hahn first traveled with NDI, he joined the staff. Currently, he serves as Director of Ambassadors and Projects.

The Worldwide Body of Christ

So in Christ we who are many form one body, and each member belongs to all the others.

Romans 12:5

For Scott Hahn, being raised in a small-town church did not give him much exposure to the worldwide body of Christ. His understanding of loving your neighbor as yourself was limited to those neighbors in which he shared the same zip code. Being a part of global missions was not on his radar.

While at college, Scott got connected with a church that spoke some about foreign missions. Still, he paid little attention to it. Imagine his surprise when in early 1999 as a soon-to-be college graduate, he was asked to accompany the pastor of the church on a mission trip to Africa.

The pastor had planned to go with NDI on a missions trip, which NDI calls *Kingdom Adventures*. The elders wanted someone from the church to accompany the pastor. As the elders prayed, one believed Scott should be the traveling companion. After the other elders confirmed this choice, Scott was asked. He agreed, thinking he would just have an enjoyable time in another country. God used the whole experience, however, to reshape Scott's life.

God provided through Scott's family and friends the exact amount needed to finance the trip with $50 leftover. While interacting with followers of Christ in Kenya, Zimbabwe, and South Africa, he saw through God's Spirit that these people truly were his spiritual brothers and sisters. Now Scott lives his life with a constant awareness of the global body of Christ, looking for ways he can serve his neighbor, be it in the same zip code or in a distant land. Playing a part in serving the worldwide body of Christ is not difficult to do. It starts with awareness. We can all pray for the growth of His church in various countries, and also give something towards furthering this growth. Some of us can even travel on short or long-term trips. What role are you playing?

Prayer

Father, help me to be aware of the needs of my brothers and sisters in Christ all around the world. Show me ways to get involved with what You are doing globally.

Making Disciples

Day 11

Singapore and Malaysia

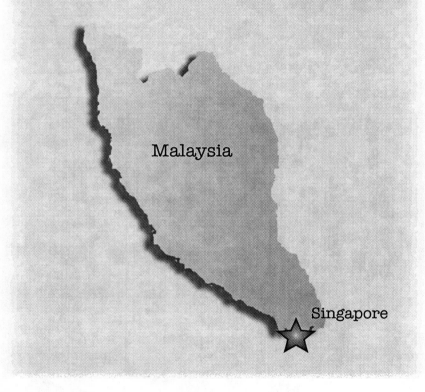

Malaysia

Singapore

Photo Description
Joseph Jabemany is the pastor of Yishun Evangelical Church in Singapore. He and his church are actively involved in planting churches in Malaysia.

Making Disciples

And the things you have heard me say in the presence of many witnesses entrust to reliable men who will also be qualified to teach others.

2 Timothy 2:2

Joseph Jabemany was born and raised on the Indian subcontinent in a traditional Hindu family. He later was exposed to the claims of Jesus Christ and came to a point where he fully trusted Christ with his life and future. As he grew in his new faith, he felt Christ directing him to serve him in pastoral ministry.

The Evangelical Church of India and Bishop Ezra Sargunam were instrumental in training and equipping Joseph for the ministry. While studying in one of their Bible schools he became fully committed to the biblical principle of following Jesus' example of discipleship. Later Joseph and his family moved to Singapore and began a church as they reached out to the Indian Diaspora there.

With his heart for discipleship, he not only discipled people in his new church but found and discipled "reliable men" in order to plant Indian churches in nearby Malaysia. As a result, God has raised up several churches under his leadership and he regularly visits them for support, training, encouragement, and edification.

It is such an exciting process, how a church is planted. An evangelist leads a family to Christ, then another family, and then another. A fellowship is started to begin to teach the new believers the basic principles of faith in Christ. They may meet indefinitely in a rented room, house, or outside under a tree. A church is born. You might not be a church planter, but Jesus can use you to teach, train, and disciple people within the sphere of influence he has given you. The biblical principle the great Apostle Paul modeled remains: be discipled first, then disciple someone else. What wonderful things God will do to build His kingdom with His discipleship multiplication process and *your* availability!

Prayer

Lord of the Harvest, please use me in these strategic days before Your return to prayerfully find people and entrust to them the concept of disciple-making.

A Chance for Childhood

Day 12

Ooty, India

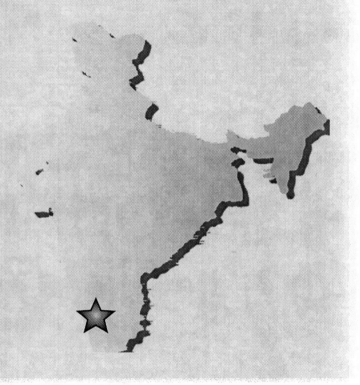

Photo Description
It is estimated that 60 million girls are "missing" in Asia, primarily due to three activities: female infanticide, prenatal sex selection, and abortion. These precious girls have a bright future thanks to the Menon family.

A Chance for Childhood

I made you grow like a plant of the field. You grew up and developed and became the most beautiful of jewels.

Ezekiel 16:7

One of the most grotesque examples of gender discrimination in the world exists in India in the form of female infanticide. Female infants are viewed as liabilities and even seen as worthless. The Hindu religion has promoted certain superstitions - that a male child is necessary to help the parents achieve the next level of reincarnation. The social custom of wedding dowries also generates a feeling of girls being a liability to parents.

Murli and Usha Menon have started a ministry in India that rescues these unwanted female babies before they are murdered. The Menons raise these girls under a new identity, one of hope and promise in Christ. The home has grown to 22 beautiful young girls, and could be exponentially larger due to the ongoing acts of murder.

Anjali was an infant whose father insisted that her mother kill her. As the mother resisted, her husband presented her with an ultimatum: "Kill the child or I will desert you." The mother heard about the Menon's work just in time and was able to save Anjali. Another baby named Nisha was abandoned on the exact day of her birth, wrapped in a cloth dipped in coconut oil. When the Menons found her, she was covered in crawling ants and had been bitten scores of times.

It is sad to think about the sin that man is capable of committing. Killing newborn babies might seem unthinkable, but it happens all the time in India. For every baby that is rescued, there are countless others that will be murdered. Pray that the Lord and His people will intervene in as many lives as possible.

Prayer

Merciful Father, please move in the hearts of parents in India who are pondering the practice of female infanticide with their daughters. Thank You for reminding me of how precious children are in Your sight.

Damaged, But Not Destroyed

Day 13

Bunia, Democratic Republic of the Congo

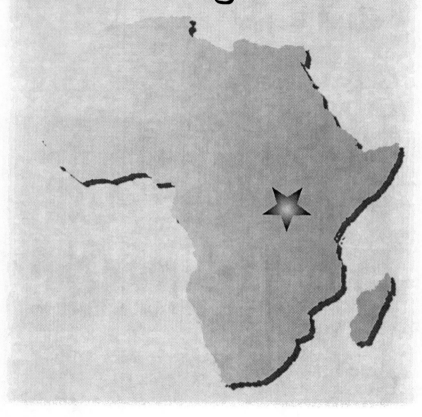

Photo Description

Bogoro Church is one of 50 churches that James Byensi has singled out as being most in need of repair or reconstruction.

Damaged, But Not Destroyed

On this rock I will build my church, and the gates of Hades will not overcome it.

Matthew 16:18

The civil war that took place in the Democratic Republic of the Congo claimed over four million lives. The country also endured clashes between the Hema and Lendu tribes. As a result, many local church buildings were severely damaged or destroyed along with other structures like schools and homes.

One of the damaged churches was Bogoro, located 25 kilometers south of the city of Bunia. The congregation had grown to around 700 members before the war. Now after the war, the people have been returning back to the village, and 70 believers have started to gather for worship in their destroyed building.

On Easter Monday, NDI Congolese Partner James Byensi assessed the damage and started the repair work. The church roof was replaced and a broken wall repaired. The pastor, believers, local chief, and military officers of the village can't find the words to share their gratitude.

Unlike the church structure, the church body was damaged, but not destroyed. Though civil war and tribal clashes scattered the believers for a season, the church building and its people are being repaired and strengthened to be a driving force in this African nation. May we also persevere in our walk with the Lord, so that nothing that comes against us will prevail. This life will be full of trials, but we can endure with God's help.

Prayer

Almighty Father, thank You for the victory You have already won over sin and death. Thank You for the comfort we have knowing that nothing can defeat the body of Christ. I pray that I would be strong in the face of anything that opposes my walk with You.

Who's in Charge Here?

Day 14

Singapore and Hong Kong

Photo Description

Woody is currently on staff with Piedmont Men of Steel after having served with NDI and Executive Ministries International (Campus Crusade for Christ).

Who's in Charge Here?

I make known the end from the beginning, from ancient times, what is still to come. I say: My purpose will stand, and I will do all that I please.

Isaiah 46:10

Woody Lamm's mother was on her way to visit her parents. As she came around a rain-slicked curve, she was violently hit and instantly killed by an eighteen-wheeler truck that had slid into her lane. Woody was only ten months old, lying in the bassinet on the front seat (this event occurred many years before child restraint seats). He was thrown through the windshield and landed face down in a drainage ditch. A lady who lived close by heard the wreck, rushed out and pulled the baby boy from the ditch, saving his life.

Woody's father was devastated, and tried unsuccessfully to drown his sorrow over the years with alcohol. As a result, Woody grew up in a very dysfunctional home. One morning when he was twelve, he discovered his father lying in a pool of blood. He had taken his life the night before. Hardened and embittered toward God and spiritual things due to his life's circumstances, Woody determined that he did not need God or anyone in his life. He would succeed on his own hard work and ingenuity.

But even as a successful young businessman, Woody found no fulfillment in his fast life of pleasure, sin, and "upward mobility." He came face-to-face with his pride and dependence on self through an evangelistic television crusade where he was marvelously converted to Jesus Christ. He later married and, after hearing God's calling into full-time Christian work, he and his wife have served well over two fulfilling decades in mission and discipleship ministries in Singapore and Hong Kong.

God has a plan and purpose for your life. Even when you don't understand it, He is daily working through all your situations for His glory. When you go through tough times, remember that God is still in charge.

Prayer

Almighty and loving Father, help me to remember that You are in control of ALL situations in this world that seem to be out of control. Help me also to daily depend on You and submit to Your plan for my life.

A Widow in Need

Day 15

Kathmandu, Nepal

Photo Description

All 15 widows living in the Elderly Home could repeat Thuli Maya Magriti's story of heartbreak and rejection – and now hope.

A Widow in Need

Religion that God our Father accepts as pure and faultless is this: to look after...widows in their distress.

James 1:27

Thuli Maya Magrati is a 76-year-old mother of 12 children and 19 grandchildren. Her husband died 35 years ago while serving in the Nepali army. In the Hindu culture, many widows are blamed for their husbands' deaths, regardless of how they died. Thuli was left to raise their children alone.

Thuli managed to see all of her children get married. Unfortunately, none of them have helped her since, and her eldest son has also died. It would have been his responsibility to care for Thuli in her old age. The hard life she has lived has taken a toll on her, and she has had several surgeries, including gall bladder surgery.

With no one to care for her, a church in Kathmandu has taken her in through an elderly home established by partners of NDI. She and 14 other precious widows get all of their needs met on a daily basis and can now live out their lives with dignity and peace. You can imagine the gratitude that these ladies have. They have been shown kindness by complete strangers in stark contrast to their own children who have abandoned them.

Is there someone, particularly a widow or widower in your neighborhood or church, who needs to receive a practical expression of the love of Christ? You can take them a meal or out to dinner, give them a book or take them to a local event. Most are lonely and just need someone to talk to.

Prayer

Father, help me to recognize the people around me, like widows, who need simple expressions of the love of Christ.

God Will Provide

Day 16

Hwange, Zimbabwe

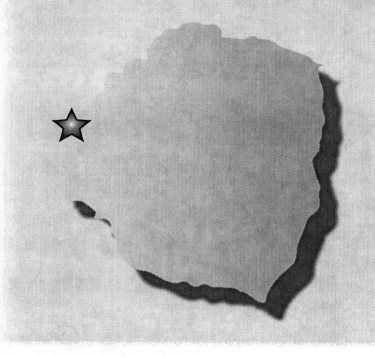

Photo Description
Maina Mkolo was such a joyful woman and a passionate speaker. Unfortunately, she died in a tragic car accident a few years ago.

God Will Provide

And my God will meet all your needs according to His glorious riches in Christ Jesus.

Philippians 4:19

Most of us here in America have never been in the difficult situation of not knowing where our next meal will come from. In so many other countries of the world, however, day-to-day survival is the norm. According to the United Nations, over 850 million people around the world are undernourished.

Simon Mkolo is an evangelist in Zimbabwe who has spent his lifetime walking from village to village preaching the Gospel. Many times he would be away from his wife, Maina, and five children for many days at a time. Money and food were often scarce, and Maina's faith was put to the test.

One day while Simon was gone, there was no food in the house to feed the family. Maina prayed to God. She believed the Lord told her to start boiling water; He would then provide the food. Very shortly thereafter, her neighbor came to the door with some extra food, ready to go in the bubbling pot. Filled with joy, this renewed Maina's faith that God would provide. This was not an isolated incident, as there were additional trying times for her that were then followed by God's gracious provision.

Have there been times in your life when your faith was put to the test? How often do you try to solve life's problems on your own before seeking the Lord? The Bible reminds us in I John 5:14-15 that we can approach God with confidence because "if we ask Him anything according to His will, He hears us. And if we know that He hears us – whatever we ask – we know that we have what we asked of Him." What reassuring words!

Prayer

Jehovah Jireh – God my Provider, thank You for meeting my needs according to Your will. I pray that my first step when I am in need is to come to You, instead of trying to do things in my own power.

The Power of Two Knees

Day 17

Les Cayes, Haiti

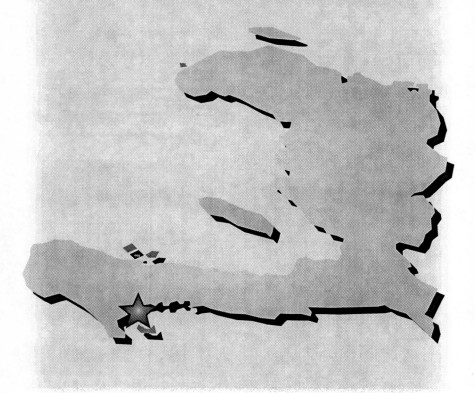

Photo Description

Chavannes Jeune finished in the top five in the most recent presidential elections in Haiti. Please pray for him as he provides much-needed spiritual leadership.

The Power of Two Knees

Humble yourselves before the Lord, and He will lift you up.

James 4:10

Pastor Chavannes Jeune is currently one of the most instrumental Christian leaders in Haiti. As a young boy, he longed for an education to better equip him for the work of the Lord, but his family could not afford it. With a literacy rate just over 50% and the average annual income at a mere $100, the odds were against Chavannes going to school and one day getting a good job.

One day after asking his father what he should do, his father told him, "You have two knees, why don't you use them?" Chavannes spent all day praying for the Lord to make a way for him to go to school.

The very next day a lost missionary team showed up in his village seeking directions to a different part of Haiti. Chavannes volunteered to take them to their destination. As a token of their appreciation, the missionary team gave him the *exact* amount that both he and his brother needed to go to school for one year!

Since then the Lord has provided a way for Chavannes to be educated even up through the university level without him having to pay for any of it himself. God also called him to the preaching ministry early in life. He preached his first open-air sermon at age nine, which resulted in 22 people surrendering to Christ!

The point of this story is not to get you to kneel when you pray. The position of your heart is more important than the position of your body. God wants you to come to Him with your needs in humility and reverential respect. He is the Almighty God who created you and cares for you. So go to Him today, confess your sins, thank Him for saving you and forgiving you, and present your requests to Him. Then "the peace of God, which transcends all understanding, will guard your hearts and minds in Christ Jesus" (Philippians 4:7).

Prayer

Father, forgive me for not talking with You more often through prayer. Forgive me of my sins. Thank You for saving me, and making me one of Your children. I know You care for me and listen to my prayers.

Tapping into God's Power

Day 18

Naxalbari, India

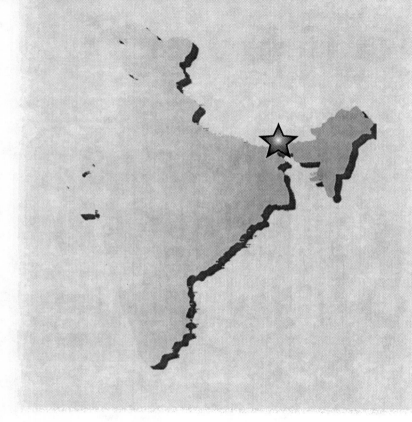

Photo Description
Dr. Suresh Sampang Rai provides medical care through mobile clinics to well over 40 villages surrounding his town.

Tapping into God's Power

In Your hands are strength and power to exalt and give strength to all.

I Chronicles 29:12

Can you imagine trying to run a hospital in rural north India *without* power? Dr. Suresh Sampang Rai had been doing so for over seven years! Before becoming a follower of Christ, he had a successful private medical practice with a secure financial future.

The Lord had other plans for Dr. Rai's life - to establish a hospital in an area where medical care was desperately needed. So he and his wife, Mary, left their comfortable life and moved to a rural area of India between Nepal and Bhutan. They began to provide care for thousands of people through a simple hospital and mobile medical clinics in dozens of surrounding villages.

Yet one important but basic necessity was missing – electricity. They had run out of their own personal funds while establishing the medical ministry, so they had no capital to put in electricity for lighting or to operate medical equipment. The Lord graciously provided through some American friends in Christ and the lights are on and the equipment is running!

Oftentimes, we go about our lives trying to do things in our own power, not going to the Father first and relying on Him. We stumble around in the darkness for long periods of time, and then wonder why life is so hard. Are there times in your life where you try to do things in your own power? Like the hospital, are you limited in

81

what you can do, because you have not tapped into the Power that is available to you?

Prayer

Forgive me, mighty God in heaven, for not relying on Your power and strength in my daily life. Help me to begin every day by asking You to be my power supply!

The God of Second Chances

PSALM 23

KAMUA, us a ersinkaaya,
wihi an 'doono tuumman
khaba.
2 Ulla inti yaakh khabto ka inas-
cha, inti bicche kijiraan ka
la iwoya.
3 Ulla miige isiiche... ro la
j'di goorat us iyl... ujiti
fissanikawoya.
4 chirri an mugai goya... so-
hdi laka, roorro ma... bo
KAMUA: j'di tahe, ati a... ji-
rta; wussaahti ersim... o
iyibta.
5 inti chiiyeey ikaagarto ka, sukuuk...
ihissa. toro la isoobahsatta m...
isubahta kokkoobeey la buu...
saggi haaggaah ichoow doon...
aah ba jiroteeytuuman il...
tan la, a garda; minkaah l...
geeddi an noolahe tuumman
soobaaya yateeh.

Day 19

83

Korr, Kenya

Photo Description
Joshua Ndooto Lengewa is standing in front of the Ten Commandments written in the Rendille language. Joshua makes sure each literacy student learns them.

The God of Second Chances

"For I know the plans I have for you," declares the Lord, "plans to prosper you and not to harm you, plans to give you hope and a future."

Jeremiah 29:11

Joshua Ndooto Lengewa was about 12 years old when he was herding goats and sheep out in the bush with the warriors of his tribe. They had made a thorn enclosure to keep the prowling hyenas and lions out. In the middle of the night, a lion jumped the homemade fence and grabbed Joshua around the waist, leapt back over the fence, and ran off into the night.

The warriors had a little dog to warn them of situations like this, and it barked constantly, waking everyone to the danger. It then ran after the lion with the warriors following. At one point, the lion dropped Joshua in order to get a better grip. The dog then harassed the lion so much and for so long, it prevented the lion from picking Joshua up again. The lion gave up and disappeared into the night. The warriors finally found Joshua thanks to the dog's barking, and put the unconscious bleeding child in the back of a truck to get him to a hospital.

Joshua spent many months in a hospital that was a day's drive from home. When he finally recovered, Joshua was able to go to a small school and get an education and at least receive one meal a day. While there, he began to learn about Jesus, and later gave his life to the Lord. Today, Joshua is the head of an outreach to the nomadic clan villages of the Rendille Tribe in the desert of Northern

Kenya through a mobile literacy program. He is a faithful and joyful man who loves the Lord and loves his people.

His story is a wonderful testimony of how God often intervenes in our lives because He has a plan for us, a plan to use us for His glory. He desires that no one die without knowing Him, often giving us second chances (or more) to give our lives to Him. Maybe there has been a time in your life when the Lord spared you, whether it was a car accident, serious illness, or an addiction of your own doing. The Lord wants to use you! Don't waste any more time before giving Him your whole life to use for His glory!

Prayer

Thank You, Father, for sparing me from an eternity of separation from You. Thank You also for the protection You have provided for me throughout my life including the times when I wasn't aware.

Living Bread

Day 20

China

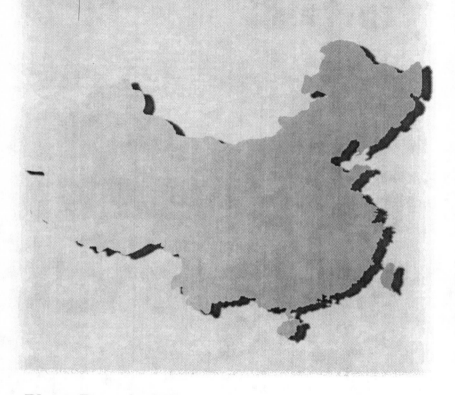

Photo Description

Pastor Yun and his family have had to go into permanent hiding as a result of his leadership and profile in the Chinese underground church.

Living Bread

Let the word of Christ dwell in you richly as you teach and admonish one another with all wisdom, and as you sing psalms, hymns and spiritual songs with gratitude in your hearts to God.

Colossians 3:16

Brother Yun decided to follow Christ after the Lord healed his father from stomach cancer. He blindly trusted in Christ to heal his father, and after witnessing that feat, Brother Yun was zealous to learn more about the true God.

Yun was told the best way to learn about Christ was from "the Holy Book from heaven." Bibles were extremely rare in China during the 1970's, so he fasted and prayed for 100 days that God would send him a Bible. The Lord showed him a vision one night of three men pushing a wheelbarrow toward Yun's house. They knocked on the door and one of the men handed Yun a package saying, "This is the living bread and you can never eat enough of this bread."

Brother Yun woke up to a knock on his door and he knew immediately that the Lord was making the vision come true and would give him a Bible. Sure enough, the vision was fulfilled.

Yun only had three years of education, so he taught himself to read using his Bible. Each day he devoured the word of God, and in a few months he had memorized the four Gospels and the book of Acts! Brother Yun has been a vital leader in the enormous house church movement in China.

For most of us, obtaining a Bible is not a difficult task. In fact we probably have multiple Bibles in our possession that are not being used. Yet there are millions of believers around the world that don't have the means to obtain a Bible for themselves. We who are fortunate to have one, do we pour ourselves into it and pour it into ourselves?

Prayer

Lord, give us a hunger for Your word. May we desire it more than the food we eat, the water we drink, and the air we breathe. Help us to realize the importance of this irreplaceable gift in our lives.

Committed to
the Cause

Day 21

Nepal

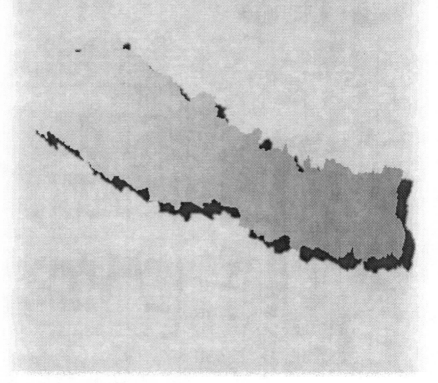

Photo Description
Joseph and Nutan Chhetri have endured quite a bit of persecution and illness over the course of their many years in ministry, but their church planting efforts successfully continue.

Committed to the Cause

Then He said to them all: "If anyone would come after me,
he must deny himself and take up his cross daily and follow Me."

Luke 9:23

In the late 1970's, Nepal was closed to the gospel, and being a believer there was hazardous to one's health. An evangelist named Joseph Chhetri had just been imprisoned for holding a prayer meeting. He was put in a cell where the sewer from the prison passed through. It was during this time that Joseph received a vision from the Lord to evangelize, plant churches, and train local Christian leaders.

After he was released, Joseph started a ministry on a local high school campus. While showing up for fellowship one day, he was unexpectedly met by a mob of 80 to 90 hostile students who drug him by his hair to the outdoor toilet and forced him into it. He was up to his chest in human waste.

For four hours the mob taunted him and demanded that he give up preaching about Christ. Joseph was urged several times to sign a document denouncing his faith, promising to never preach again. Each time he refused. Each time he was beaten until he was unconscious.

It was after awakening from one of the final beatings that Joseph cried out to the Lord to take his life because he could endure no more. His attackers were so moved by his commitment to Christ that many of them began weeping with him and he was set free. It took 15 days of bed rest for Joseph to recover from that tortuous day.

Joseph is now working in northern India where he has planted 12 churches in previously unreached areas, predominantly among the tea plantation workers.

Persecution is taking place on a global scale. Pray that followers of Christ have the strength to endure. You must also stand up for your faith with people you know. While you may not face severe consequences yet, you must boldly stand nonetheless.

Prayer

Lord, carrying the cross is a high and holy calling, but not an easy one. Uphold me during the times when it is most difficult to deny myself for the cause of Christ.

What Might Have Been

Day 22

Monrovia, Liberia

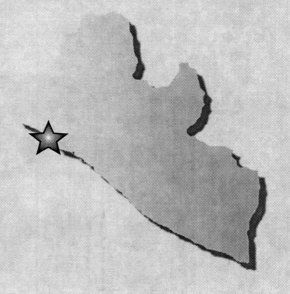

Photo Description

Praise the Lord that Marcia accepted the Lord and was baptized by her father before becoming ill and going to heaven. John and Martha have four other children and care for other relatives as well.

What Might Have Been

He will defend the afflicted among the people and save the children of the needy.

Psalm 72:4

While Liberia was going through civil war, John and Martha Partor lived with their five children in a refugee camp in the neighboring country of Guinea. In 2004 they were able to return with their children to Liberia and settle in the capital of Monrovia.

Life has not been easy for the Partors, especially for their oldest daughter, Marcia. For ten years, Marcia struggled with stabilizing diabetes. She began to have kidney problems, develop an enlarged heart, and lose her eyesight. John and Martha tried unsuccessfully to get their diabetic daughter to the U.S. for proper medical care.

Marcia never got the proper treatment. As her condition worsened, they were so preoccupied with the diabetes, they realized too late that she was severely dehydrated. This combined with the inability to have the proper diet and medication resulted in Marcia dying before finishing her final year of high school. The Partors are left to rest in God's sovereignty, but wonder what might have been had Marcia gotten the help she needed.

Health care is something we often take for granted. We may complain about waiting in emergency rooms for a few hours or the cost of a prescription. At least care and treatment are readily available. As John shared, Marcia's struggle is an example of "why most African kids die earlier from some of these manageable sicknesses and diseases."

Be thankful for the many blessings God has given us in this great country. Show your appreciation by praying for the millions of children like Marcia who don't get the medical care they need.

Prayer

Thank you, Father, for blessing America in so many ways. Most of our needs are met with so little effort. Please help the families around the world who don't have access to proper medical care. Provide a way to save their children from disease and premature death.

A New Creation

Day 23

Nairobi, Kenya

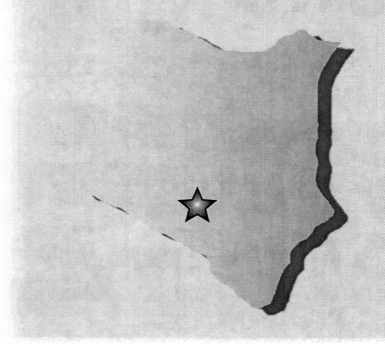

Photo Description
Timothy Mulehi walks with Scott Hahn in the Kibera slums
of Nairobi, Kenya. About one million people live in two
square miles.

A New Creation

Therefore, if anyone is in Christ, he is a new creation;
the old has gone, the new has come!

II Corinthians 5:17

Timothy Mulehi was a drunk. He tried to find satisfaction in alcohol and in running around, but found there was nothing that made him feel better. Countless times, he would go to bed very dizzy and drunk, and then wake up countless times with hangovers. One day he was drinking in a bar in his native country of Kenya. A man in the bar got up in his face with a gun because he believed that Timothy was making a pass at his girlfriend. He never pulled the trigger, but it really scared Timothy. He went home and starting thinking about his life. If he had been shot and killed, where would he be then?

Not long after, the Lord brought a missionary into Timothy's life to share the Gospel with him. It was the first time he had ever heard about sin, hell, and the love of God. He knelt down, confessed his sins, and became a new creation.

Timothy left his drunken ways behind, and today, he is a pastor, gifted evangelist, and director of a program that cares for and educates 700 street children in the slums of Nairobi, Kenya. He is a bold witness for Christ in these slums and has a wonderful testimony to share with his people, proudly proclaiming, "I was born in the slums. I will die in the slums."

We all have sins in our past that we need to let die with our old self. If we have received salvation from the Lord, we need to "throw off everything that hinders and the sin that entangles" as it says in Hebrews 12:1. It is hard to throw off these sins from our old life. But the Lord can give you the victory over these sins so you can throw them off for good!

Prayer

Creator of the heavens and earth, thank You that You have made me a new creation. Help me invest myself in worthy ministry for You. And if any bad habits linger, remove them permanently from my life.

Random Act of Kindness

Day 24

Carrefour, Haiti

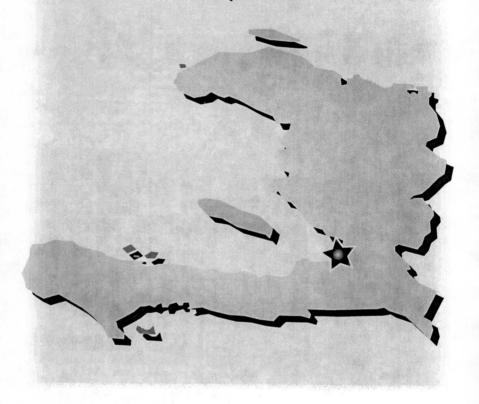

Photo Description
To date, Crawford Hitt has overseen the distribution of more than 16,000 Edu-Packs in ten countries.

Random Act of Kindness

*Show mercy and compassion to one another. Do not oppress the
widow or the fatherless, the alien or the poor.*

Zechariah 7:9-10

Haiti is often described as the most impoverished
nation in the Western Hemisphere. Prior to Crawford
Hitt's first trip into the country, he had read all of
the information he could about Haiti. The more
he traveled on that first trip, the less he saw of the
poverty, and the more he saw of a proud people struggling against
all odds.

While on the trip, Crawford's team handed out gifts of shoes,
clothes, hospital supplies, and toys to random needy children that
they came across. There was always a multitude following them
that was orderly, but anxious to get something before the team ran
out of whatever was being given away. During these distributions, a
defining moment took place for Crawford in the city of Carrefour.

The team was down to handing out small three-inch by five-inch
spiral notepads and golf pencils. Crawford was embarrassed that
they were even giving these particular supplies away. "Who would
want this," he silently thought. "It was something we would just
throw in a drawer and forget."

As soon as the children saw what was being given away, they
rushed the jeep, practically crawling over each other to get their
own pencils and pads, exclaiming, "Now we can got to school!" In
that moment God galvanized Crawford's heart to start Edu-Pack, a

ministry arm of NDI that collects and sends school supplies to needy children around the world.

It was a joy for Crawford's team to do these random acts of kindness for children who least expected it. You have the opportunity to be kind to children and others as well - right where you live. Take some time to do a random act of kindness for someone today.

Prayer

Father, just as You have showered me with mercy and compassion, help me to do the same for those around me. Show me creative ways to bless others with acts of kindness.

God's Calling

Day 25

Mfensi, Ghana

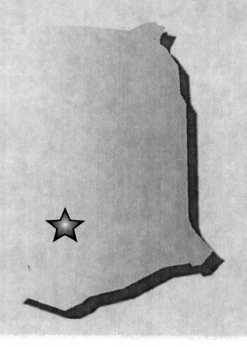

Photo Description
Yaw Asante's main resources for evangelism are a conference center and farm.

God's Calling

I urge you to live a life worthy of the calling you have received.

Ephesians 4:1

Yaw Asante started out to be trained as a science teacher in his native land of Ghana, but soon found out that he could not escape the calling of God on his life to become an evangelist and pastor trainer. Yaw had been raised in the church in rural Ghana and had surrendered his life to Christ while in high school. Once he became true to his calling, God showed him many open doors for ways of better equipping himself for the future ministry God had planned for him.

Daystar University College in Kenya, and later, the *Conference for Itinerant Evangelists* in Amsterdam, provided excellent biblical tools and principles for Yaw's development. He threw himself into both preaching the Gospel in his native land as well as training other evangelists and pastors to be self-sufficient. His ministry philosophy is called "The 3 'M' Concept of Gospel Ministry." This philosophy is comprised of Meditation (spiritual), Marketplace (manual work), and Ministering (outward focus).

Tribal groups along the Ghana/Burkina Faso border are now experiencing the fruit of Yaw's training. He is working with these groups that are comprised of about 80% African religions and 20% Islamic. This strategic focus is based upon trying to reach tribal people before the Muslims attempt to convert them. By being true to his calling Yaw is now sharing the life-changing truth about Jesus Christ to those that God brings into his path.

God has called everyone to be His witnesses, but do you know what your specific spiritual gifts are? Determining what they are will help you serve the Lord in the most effective way. Most churches have access to some type of spiritual gifts inventory test that can get you started on the path of using your gifts for God's glory.

Prayer

Giver of every good and perfect gift, please keep me greatly aware of the wonderful spiritual gifts you have given me. Help me to use these gifts in ways that would glorify You in the greatest way possible.

Availability and Obedience

Day 26

Nawalparasi District, Nepal

Photo Description
In addition to planting churches, Dil Tamang has become
self-supporting through a bee-keeping project funded by NDI
partners. He is a major seller of honey in his district.

Availability and Obedience

My grace is sufficient for you, for My power is made perfect in weakness.

II Corinthians 12:9

Dil Tamang is a cripple. He has to use a cane to walk the rough and mountainous terrain of Nepal. It would be easy for him to tell the Lord that he was not qualified to witness to his people. Yet after Dil became a follower of Christ, he yielded to the Lord's call.

Dil has experienced the joys of finding a wife and raising three children, and has endured over three years in prison for his faith. He also became an elder in a church that has now planted well over 75 daughter churches! After several years of service to this church, he felt compelled to go back to his home district and share the Gospel. As a result of this crippled man's witness, several more churches have been planted as well as some house fellowships.

Do you have a physical weakness or trait that you use as an excuse not to serve God? Are you like Moses, who didn't feel qualified because of a speech impediment? Are you like Abraham, who thought he was too old for the Lord to work in his life?

The Lord wants to use you no matter what your weaknesses may be. The Bible states that when you are weak, God is strong. Jesus surrounded Himself with people who weren't "qualified" to evangelize. Look at the disciples – among them were fishermen, a tax collector, and a revolutionary. Yet the Lord used them to launch His salvation message to the whole world.

You are saved because these men were obedient to the call, so you too should be available to God for His service, then obedient when He gives direction - just like Dil. It will be the hardest but most rewarding journey you will ever experience!

Prayer

Thank You, Lord, for using me in spite of my sins and shortcomings. I am making myself available for You to work through me. Help me to develop a willing and obedient heart.

It Takes Courage

Day 27

Timbuktu, Mali

Photo Description
Nouh Yattara is considered the foremost Christian leader in the Muslim north of Mali. Despite living among fundamental Muslims, his witness is as bold as ever.

It Takes Courage

Be strong and courageous. Do not be afraid or terrified because of them, for the Lord your God goes with you; He will never leave you nor forsake you.

Deuteronomy 31:6

It's tough being a follower of Christ in a country with less than a one percent evangelical population. Such is the case in the Muslim country of Mali. It's even tougher when no one else in your family is a believer either.

When Pastor Nouh Yattara was a young boy, he secretly went to a Bible Camp without his family's permission. When he returned home, his father was so mad that he tied Nouh up for a week without food or water, asking him to deny Christianity. Nouh said, "Father, I am ready to do anything you want to show you how much I am ready to obey. But I cannot deny Jesus Christ because I found in Him peace and joy that I do not want to lose."

At the end of the week, relatives and neighbors came to talk in Nouh's favor to his father. His father had the right to kill him according to the teachings of Islam, but they wanted Nouh's life spared. They succeeded in sparing his life, but his father said, "Leave my home. I deny you as my son. If you come back, I will kill you." Nouh then left and lived with a Christian couple for the next two years. Today, Nouh is a pastor and has led several of his family members to the Lord.

It takes great courage to stand up for your faith like Nouh did to his father. Here in America you don't face this kind of persecution.

But there have probably been countless times that you have had the opportunity to stand up for your faith in a situation where the truth should be heard.

God gives us daily opportunities to be salt and light on this earth (Matthew 5:13-16), whether it's standing in the grocery line, getting gas for your car, or eating at a restaurant. Take courage and stand up for your faith!

Prayer

Father, help me to recognize when You are presenting opportunities for me to share my faith with others. Please also protect and strengthen those who courageously put their lives on the line for Your sake.

Off Track

Day 28

Addis Ababa, Ethiopia

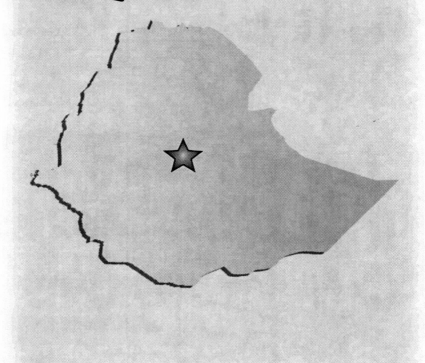

Photo Description

Even though half of the population is Orthodox like this
priest and another third is Muslim, Ethiopia is ripe for the
Gospel *(NDI partner's identity not shown for his protection)*.

Off Track

*If you confess with your mouth, "Jesus is Lord," and believe in
your heart that God raised Him from the dead, you will be saved.*

Romans 10:9

While the church in Ethiopia can trace its roots
back to the Ethiopian eunuch who was reached
by Philip in Acts 8:26-39, it has gotten deeply
off track in the two thousands years that followed his conversion.

The Ethiopian Orthodox Church is steeped in culture and
tradition, using books based on legend rather than the Bible. Among
their faulty doctrines is that salvation comes from good deeds - a
belief that many people in the Western World seem to embrace as
well.

One of NDI's partners has a burden to reach these priests with
the lifesaving message of Christ. He is discreetly giving Bibles to
orthodox priests and training them in the true Word of God.

Going to church or even volunteering and serving in the church
does not mean you are saved and going to heaven. Doing good
deeds doesn't get you there either. You must believe in your heart
and confess with your mouth that Jesus died on the cross for your
sins, and was raised from the dead to so that you might live with
Him throughout eternity.

Are you or someone you know believing the lie that you must
earn your way into heaven? Do you know that God's love is
unconditional once you embrace what He's done for you? Be sure

121

you understand what the Bible clearly does say and does not say instead of getting your Christian beliefs from any other source.

Prayer

Gracious heavenly Father, please guide me through Your Word into knowledge of the truth. I confess with my mouth and believe in my heart that You raised Your Son from the dead. Thank You for saving me and for extending Your unconditional love to me.

Where to Focus

Day 29

Dambulla, Sri Lanka

Photo Description

Somawathi (at left) has opened up her home to the local church for prayer meetings and worship.

Where to Focus

But seek first His kingdom and His righteousness, and all these things will be given to you as well.

Matthew 6:33

There is no proper roof, and no doors or windows in Somawathi's simple little hut in Dambulla village near Kandalama, Sri Lanka. There isn't any furniture or electricity. There is no water nearby and this area is very dry, so it is very difficult during the dry season, as she has to walk far to get clean drinking water. There is no toilet, only a small space covered by cardboard. Somawathi is living in the most basic of conditions along with 15 other families in her village who live in similar circumstances.

As if life wasn't challenging enough, Somawathi is a widow, and life has been hard; she can only find part-time work cleaning houses. She has been a follower of Christ for five years, and is attending a house fellowship in Kandalama with her son. Despite her struggle to survive, Somawathi believes that the Lord is looking out for her.

One of our joys of working in full-time ministry is getting to be a conduit of blessing to someone like Somawathi. An NDI domestic partner came forward to provide the needed funds for a home for her. It only cost $1,500 to construct a simple room and toilet for Somawathi and her son.

The above passage in Matthew 6 reminds us that we do not need to worry about the basic necessities of life like food, water, and clothing. Our heavenly Father knows we need them. Therefore, we should focus on doing His will and let Him provide for our needs as they arise.

Prayer

Father, thank You for caring for me so deeply that I don't have to worry about my needs – especially in a great country like America. You knew what I needed before I was even born. Remind me to keep focused on serving You, and in some way, small or great, be used to relieve the suffering of another person.

A Love with No Boundaries

Day 30

India

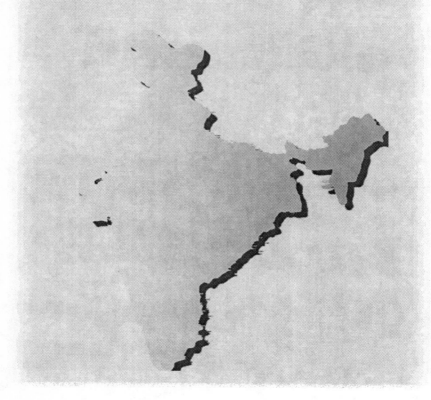

Photo Description
The Dalits and tribals are the forgotten people of India - forgotten, that is, by everyone but the body of Christ.

A Love with No Boundaries

For I am convinced that neither death nor life, neither angels nor demons, neither the present nor the future, nor any powers, neither height nor depth, nor anything else in all creation, will be able to separate us from the love of God that is in Christ Jesus our Lord.

Romans 8:38-39

Amerian society has a history of segregating itself along racial and monetary lines. The Hindu caste system, on the other hand, segments Indian society in an even more pronounced way into very distinct and different levels. The highest caste is the *Brahmins* who are the teachers and priests of Hinduism. Second is the *Kshatriyas* who are the warriors. Next is the *Vaishyas* or tradesmen. Then, there are the *Shudras*, the laborers.

Below them are two groups that comprise one fourth of India's population. One group is called *Dalits*, previously known as "untouchables." They are generally constrained to do the menial dirty jobs that no one else will do, and deal with extreme social segregation. They are the poorest of the poor and are not allowed to interact with people in the higher castes. At the very bottom of the social spectrum are the dehumanized people called *tribals*, who have been living in the jungles and hills for generations, surviving on hunting and rain-dependent farming using primitive methods.

In the midst of a hopeless situation, a tremendous movement is taking place among the Dalits and the tribals, as many of them are having their eyes opened to the freedom and hope offered to them through Christ. It should be of no surprise that this is taking place, for the love of Jesus Christ reaches out to all people and knows no boundaries. Though their fellow countrymen have abandoned them, the Dalits and tribals find unconditional acceptance in the family of God.

As a follower of Christ, you should find it comforting that God loves you no matter who you are or what your social status is. Thank him today for His *unconditional* love. Also, there are friends and family from all levels of society that need to grasp the infinite love that God has for them. Pray that the Lord would give you the words to share this truth with them.

Prayer

Thank You for loving me unconditionally, Father. It is so comforting to know that nothing can separate me from Your love. Help me to share that same love with others.

Finishing the Race

Day 31

Nepal and Tibet

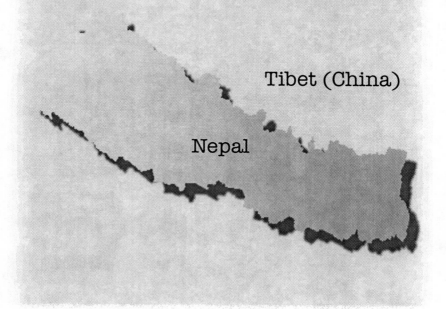

Tibet (China)

Nepal

Photo Description

Both within and outside the Tibetan community, Nima
Tshering is affectionately called *Pala*, which means father.
He is greatly respected, and rightfully so.

Finishing the Race

However, I consider my life worth nothing to me, if only I may finish the race and complete the task the Lord Jesus has given me – the task of testifying to the gospel of God's grace.

Acts 20:24

Western culture paints an enticing dream of working hard for a long season so you can retire to a life of enjoyment. Golfing, fishing, shopping, or social activities often characterize the picturesque life of retirement. Little emphasis is placed, even in Christian circles, on continuing to work to build the Kingdom of God once retirement age is reached. Thankfully, Nima Tshering did not follow the norm.

Nima leads one of the oldest known – if not the oldest – Tibetan ministries founded and run by Tibetans. It is located in the Kathmandu Valley overlooking the Himalayan Mountains of Nepal. Many Tibetans come to settle here, if they survive the trek over the mountains. *Champa Choeling* or "Place of Love" is the name of Nima's ministry, which is making an impact particularly on many Tibetan refugee children.

At one time Nima was a Buddhist monk studying under the Dalai Lama in Tibet before Christ claimed Nima for His glory. He has now passed along the Christian faith within his family to the third generation. He has also written many Tibetan hymns and praise songs. Perhaps his crowning achievement culminated in 2002 when, at the age of 84, Nima finished a 14-year project of translating the Old Testament into the common Tibetan language.

Praise God for Nima Tshering who did not retire from life when he reached an age to retire from work. God can use you no matter what your age. Some of your best years of service to Him can take place after you retire from your vocation. The world needs older and wiser people to guide us!

Prayer

Lord, help me to realize that You have called me to serve in Your Kingdom all of my life, regardless of my employment. Reveal to me now how I can best serve You until I finish my life on earth.

Conclusion

I hope that this devotional journey you've taken in the last month has blessed, encouraged, and motivated you to become actively involved in the Lord's work. It's easier than you might think.

There are four simple ways you can be a part of what God is doing:

- **You can pray.** Praying daily for lost souls is perhaps the most important weapon in your spiritual arsenal, and will give you a global heart and mindset. It also provides the prayer cover that is so desperately needed in areas that are unreached or hostile to the message of Christ. Develop a simple monthly prayer calendar that lists things to pray for daily, such as unsaved family members or those who are sick.

- **You can give.** I encourage you to deploy your tithes and offerings in the most effective way possible. Hopefully, your church is actively involved in missions. If not, there are numerous organizations that would welcome your financial partnership. Be sure to investigate their Statement of Faith and understand their accounting practices.

- **You can go.** Seeing what the Lord is doing firsthand in some place outside of your comfort zone and country can be one of the most rewarding experiences you will ever have. You will meet amazing people – like the ones you've just read about – with incredible testimonies who are giving their very lives to share the love of Christ with people.

- **You can share**. You have a story that others need to hear. The events, struggles, and triumphs of your life will bless and encourage others. You can also share about what the Lord is doing around the world. From one-on-one to your Bible study group to your workplace, sharing with others doesn't have to be some formal speech or take place at some official event. Everyday life is where sharing most easily happens.

You are on a mission. It is Christ's Great Commission, to go out from your front door into the world and share your life and testimony with others. It's not complicated. Just be yourself. God wants to use you and your gifts. He doesn't want you to try and be someone else. He has uniquely gifted you to serve Him and serve others. The sooner you realize this and make yourself available to Him, the sooner your life will be filled with joy and eternal purpose. Are you ready to answer His call?

New Directions International
Reaching the Unreached through Partnership

New Directions International is an evangelical missions organization that connects followers of Christ with strategic leaders overseas to help fulfill the Great Commission. We have a particular emphasis on Christian leaders who are sharing God's love with unreached and under-reached people groups. We partner with them primarily through four initiatives:

- **Training Leaders**
  Pastors and evangelists overseas are thirsty for Bible teaching to equip them in their efforts to evangelize and disciple their people.

- **Building Churches**
  A permanent physical structure is crucial to the stability and growth of the congregation, often doubling their size after only a few years after construction is completed

- **Educating Children**
  Through *Edu-Pack* children are given backpacks full of the supplies they need to go to school. Also through feeding and literacy programs, needy children are helped in spiritual and practical ways.

- **Initiating Self-Support**
  A small business or micro enterprise like a tractor, shop or vehicle will earn the necessary income for a leader's family to support themselves, allowing them to more fully concentrate on their ministry

NDI has received a 4-Star rating (out of 4 stars) by Charity Navigator, America's largest independent evaluator of charities, for 2005 and 2006.

> *Only 12% of the charities we've rated have received at least two consecutive 4-star evaluations, indicating that New Directions International outperforms most charities in America in its efforts to operate in the most fiscally responsible way possible. This 'exceptional' designation from Charity Navigator differentiates New Directions International from its peers and demonstrates to the public it is worthy of their trust.*

Trent Stamp
Executive Director
Charity Navigator

A higher standard.
A higher purpose.

NDI is annually audited by an independent public accounting firm. Our financial statements are available upon request. NDI is a member of the Evangelical Council for Financial Accountability: **www.ecfa.org**.

How *You* Can Get Involved with NDI

Join our email and mailing list

We would love to keep you informed about all of the exciting ministry activities of NDI. Through our bimonthly newsletter and semi-monthly email updates, you'll stay in touch with what is going on around the world. Sign up online today!

Pray for the ministry

By becoming a Prayer Partner with NDI, you are providing us with your most important activity – your

prayers. Using our quarterly Prayer Calendar, you can pray for NDI on a daily basis.

Go on a *Kingdom Adventure*

A *Kingdom Adventure* is an overseas missions trip with NDI. You get to see firsthand what God is doing to build His Kingdom while also being exposed to natural wonders and different cultures.

Be an Ambassador

If you have a passion for one or more of our four primary areas of ministry, we'll give you the tools necessary to represent this need in your sphere of influence.

Become a member of
Circle of Friends

Our ministry needs domestic partners who give $25 or more on a monthly basis to help NDI function as a ministry, so that we can then focus our time and efforts on helping to fulfill the Great Commission.

Equip our Overseas Partners

Getting financially involved in training leaders, building churches, educating children, and initiating self-support can be done with a gift of $10 or more. Visit our website for more details.

www.newdirections.org

About the Author

Joseph L. Williams grew up in a strong mission-minded family, and took many summer trips to the country of Haiti. His father, Dr. J.L. Williams, founded New Directions International (NDI) in 1968.

Joseph graduated from Appalachian State University with a degree in Communications in 1995. Since that time, Joseph has been in full-time mission work with NDI, most recently as Vice President of Marketing and International Ministries.

Cumulatively, he has spent well over a year of his life taking more than 36 short-term mission trips to over 27 countries. He met his wife, Susannah Wesley Morris, while helping lead a youth work team to Haiti in 1995.

Joseph currently resides in Graham, North Carolina, with Susannah and their two children, Nathanael and Abigail. His first book, entitled *Hardship, Healing, and Hope: How God Still Moves in the Lives of His People*, was released by VMI Publishers in May 2007.

Available on Amazon, Walmart, Books-A-Million, and Barnes & Noble's websites

www.josephlwilliams.net

About the Founder

Dr. J.L. Williams is currently serving as Chief Ministry Officer of New Directions International, the organization he founded in 1968 in Burlington, North Carolina.

J.L. graduated from Asbury College with a pre-med major, from Duke Divinity School with a Master of Divinity degree in comparative world religions, and from Luther Rice Seminary with a Doctor of Ministry degree in contemporary counter-Christian cults.

During the early years when J.L. led New Directions with his wife, Patt, the ministry was an interdenominational and interracial singing group comprised of high school and college students. They were pioneers in using contemporary Christian music to share their faith in churches, schools, prisons, street corners, malls, beaches, or anywhere they could find an audience. Traveling on weekends during the school year and throughout the vacation months, they ended each summer with a cross-cultural mission trip.

Those intense and varied experiences of discipleship, practical evangelism, and mission outreaches became the training ground for many young men and women who went on to actively minister in various denominations and parachurch organizations. Eventually, the focus shifted from mentoring American teenagers and college-age young people to equipping pastors and Christian leaders in countries overseas – the primary focus of the ministry today.

J.L. and Patt live in Burlington, North Carolina, have four married children, and 10 grandchildren.

Do you need a
mission's project?

Edu-Pack provides backpacks full of essential school supplies for needy children here at home and around the world. These children are shown the love of Christ through the distribution of this practical yet effective tool.

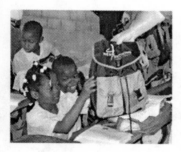

How you can be involved:

- Corporately as a church
- Missions Committee
- Sunday School Classes
- Youth Group
- Vacation Bible School
- Seniors Group
- Individually

Just fill a bag full of school supplies and enclose $10 to cover the costs of distribution (for a list of appropriate items, visit www.edu-pack.org). Or give $20, and we will fill and distribute the backpack for you.

Get started today!

NEW DIRECTIONS
INTERNATIONAL

ECFA
MEMBER

Notes

Notes

~~Annilise~~
Annelise
HOUSTON ST.
38801